Disappearance

Lesley Harrison

Disappearance

—north sea poems—

Shearsman Books

First published in the United Kingdom in 2020 by
Shearsman Books
P.O. Box 4239
Swindon
SN3 9FN

Shearsman Books Ltd Registered Office
30–31 St. James Place, Mangotsfield, Bristol BS16 9JB
(this address not for correspondence)

www.shearsman.com

ISBN 978-1-84861-698-1

Copyright © Lesley Harrison, 2020

The right of Lesley Harrison to be identified as the author of this work has been asserted by her in accordance with the Copyrights, Designs and Patents Act of 1988.
All rights reserved.

CONTENTS

Birds of the North Sea	9
Barnacle	10
Topophilia	11
Close's Fishermen's Map	15
Passing Place	22
Orkney Road Trip with Samuel Beckett	23
Spate	26
February, Montrose Basin	28
Crossing the Pentland	31
The Voyage of the 'Fox'	32
Littoral ~ rune poems	40
Birds of Angus	41
Votive Ships	42
Thursday Poem	45
Crovie	46
December, Skagaströnd	49
Lizzie Fairy	55
Hessle Road	56
Hull	62
Disappearance	65
Burnhead	74
notes	76

Fare forward, voyagers!
All old men are explorers.

BIRDS OF THE NORTH SEA

An invocation, using birds' names as they alter during passage or along migration routes between Orkney, Shetland, the Faroe Islands, Iceland and Svalbard. To be read aloud.

arctic skua	tyvjo – aulin – kjove – kjói -tyvjo
arctic tern	ritto – tirrick – kría -kyst
black guillemot	teistie – tystie – tjest – peiste -teist
curlew	whaup – whaap –wulp
golden plover	weeo – hjejle – ló – heilo
great northern diver	emmer – immer gös – imbre – lómr –islom
gull	meeuw – maa – måge – máfur -måke
lapwing	kievit – teeick – whippo –vibe
long tailed duck	ijseend - calloo - havelle –hávella
oystercatcher	skeldro – shalder – tjaldr –chaldro
razorbill	alk – wylkie – álka – alle -apparluk
ringed plover	sanloo – sinlick – sandiloo –sandlo

BARNACLE
In *Topographia Hibernica* (1187), Gerald of Wales described
how he had seen geese hatching from mollusc shells.

like seaweeds attaching to timber,
wherein are these little lung creatures
all pendicle and mouthing

their hard beards filtering the tide,
a mouth cone, a soft sack of eggs
a dark bead, dormant, suspended;

until they split from their stump,
sleeking out ungloved
– half milt, half gargoyle –

and dive joyfully into the air, growing full
and certain, their pinbones ripening
creaking past in long, dry lines

dispersing in the vast
blind margin of the ocean.
Thus they become themselves at last.

TOPOPHILIA
*Saint Cuthbert (c. 634 – 687) spent his last years in seclusion
in a cell on the Northumbrian island of Inner Farne.*

i.
morning.
a cloud lifts, the island resolving
in a turn of ocean

the sparkling clink of waves on sand
sound, a living matter
sound illumined

a wave swallowing a rock pool,
the gulls, their sharp words
repeated and repeated

the god of my childhood
in the grey white sea noise
in the screech of seabirds.

ii.
Spring tide.
I walk into the sea's cold bloom,
its heft, its anonymity.

I trace my entire belief
in the viscera of salt and wind,
the natural fall of cloud.

here is only everything:
the secular ocean,
the crush and crush of new waves;

its motion brings peace,
the beach, its privacy and darkness
a relief from psalmody.

iii.
a round hull
knocking into hollows

the eider,
their broody pots of down

this bright space,
its salutary emptiness.

iv.
a stone cell
hunkered on a rock.
quiet vacancy.

v.
gathering
in the green light of dawn

eider croon in the
hollows between waves

their white defined by
the darkness of thewater

conscious points
in this inexhaustible space.

vi.
to dwell outside myself,
to live in the lived world
among snails and grasses

in ordinary daylight
growing old, neither man nor woman
fasting in silence.

vii.
the dune slacks. beds of neat helleborine
watercress and elder.
the milk vetch, tight lipped.

viii.
otters pry in bedrock
puddling the sand, then vanishing completely
in the heavy green.

I love the disappearance –
the free power of waves,
the world that ends at the surface

the presences of stars in daylight.
the thin white moon.
the gannets, their slow ovation.

CLOSE'S FISHERMEN'S CHART. SECTION 2. THE NORTH SEA.
London: Edward Stanford, 1905. Price 10/-

Coming from the westward
a ship enters the true stream

the true stream will always carry a vessel
towards the North Foreland
, and from it when it is falling

except near the Coasts, where
it partakes the form of the land

THE SEA BED

When taking soundings, it **mu**st be borne in mind, that the sea be**d**, like the land, consists of hills, valleys, plains of sand or **mu**d ; of rugged cliffs, sometimes with abrupt faces, at others with jagged sloping sides, or strewn with boulders, etc.,etc. A single cast of lead might mislea**d** a mariner, as it might happen to drop on a spot either much more shoal, or much deeper than the average sounding**s** in the neighbourhood. This explains why fishermen find many soundings not shown on any chart.

Fi**sh**ermen sound every yard of the sea under 200 fathoms in depth, and find nearly every shoal, reef, or deep hole in the sea. A Gove**r**nment surveying ship out at sea, only sounds a spot **h**ere and there, as a rule many miles apart. The distances can easily be as**c**ertained by following the line of soundage and measuring the distance between each.

Note carefully the distance between the soundings on the chart you are using, and then plot your soundings a**c**cordingly on the chart. Experience has demon**st**rated that as a rule a series of soundings plotted on a chart at the same distance, agree within a fathom or two with those shown on a chart, even in deep water. In the case of a very foul bottom, the difference in the soundings may be even greater. But a navigator in such cases will of **c**ourse use his commonsense.

*mud, dark, sand, shells, rock, hole, course, stones

– ABERDEEN BANK – Buchan Deep – WITCH GROUND – SWATCHWAY –
THE GAT – LONG FORTIES *Fine Sand* –

WITCH HOLE

>they leaned towards Denmark
>divining the grey ship,
>eyes hair streaming
>
>moaning like gulls,
>boiling cloud out of
>a blue ordinary morning,
>
>the new queen
>buckled, puking in the squall
>waves fizzing
>
>at the keel –
>the white bloom of water that
>the ship fell through.

UNST

>this island
>where grass grows like hair.
>
>on days like this
>you breathe through your skin.

THE GAT

gåos - tirrick - mallimak - svartbakr
Those lost at sea come back as birds.

– St MAGNUS GROUND – TURBOT BANK *Rough* – OTTER BANK SPRING & SUMMER HALIBUT. COD.LING. WHEN CLEAR OF DOGFISH –

ST MAGNUS GROUND

snow falls
on the dark moor

the old ship groaning
like a tree.

NUN'S ROCK

kneeling to bedrock –
entranced

almost overshadowed in the
sudden sea hole

biblically black,
her blunt head – her cowl – her silence

OUTER BAILEY

    a dozen petrels
    low to the water

    almost landing   pattering the
    constant downslide,

THE MINCHES

        afterwards,

    the sky
    blue as a boat.

    – SANDHAILE FLATS – WELL HOLE – OUTER WELL BANK
    – OUTER SILVER PIT – DOGGER BANK SW PATCH {*Breaks in strong gales*

SILVER PITS

    fog: blind ahead.
    large areas of silence,

    a loose fluorescence
    that turns to ash or dust

as if about to snow.
a slight sea falls, and falls

FARN DEEPS

the moon, occluded.

a single bulb
hung in the belly of the kirk

DOGGER BANK

sīc (Old English)   *slakki (Old Norse)*
sík (Old Norse)   *slack (Yorkshire)*
sig (Danish)   *slug (Angus)*
sike (Yorkshire)   *sluch (Shetland, North East)*
syke (Berwick)   *sloc (Gaelic)*

– TAIL END DOGGER BANK – NORTH EAST PIT –
SYLT GROUND – HELIGOLAND DEEPS – BORKUM
FLAT – OYSTER BEDS –

WADDEN SEA

strange dreamland,
this subtidal region:

sea to bay
bay to lake
lake to swamp

swamp to weak meadow
the old seabed
brought up to the air

the wind blowing carefully all day,
the ground so dry
that walking is easy.

HELIGOLAND

September.
a sharp cold stream
a pink line of current

the wind from the moon
kindling the sky
green   then coral red.

two or three stars
glow   low down
like aeroplanes, landing.

THE SEA BED

                                        the   the

                                                  the

　the

                          the

                                    the

    the   the
        the

                                              the

            the

PASSING PLACE
the B974

Meet me in a fold of hills
of waterlight and stone,
with broken daylight following
the silver levels down.

We'll wash the morning into blue
and cloud the hills with sun;
then swallow dance on empty air,
my shadow child, my one.

We'll weave the grasses into hours,
and when the hours are gone
I'll gather up my coat of earth
and take the road alone.

ORKNEY ROAD TRIP WITH SAMUEL BECKETT

Sometimes it's the sea, other times the mountains, often it was the forest, the city, the plain too, I've flirted with the plain too, I've given myself up for dead all over the place
'Texts for Nothing'

the A9 at Halberry Head, Caithness

Suddenly, no, at last, long last, I couldn't any more, I couldn't go on. Someone said, You can't stay here. I couldn't stay there and I couldn't go on. I'll describe **the place** that's unimportant. The top, very flat, of **a mountain, no, a hill**, but so wild, so wild, enough. **Quag, heath** up to the knees, faint sheep-tracks, troughs scooped deep by the rains. It was **far down** in one of these I was lying, out of the wind. Glorious prospect, but for **the** mist that blotted out everything, valleys, loughs, plain and **sea**. How can I go on, I shouldn't have begun, no, I had to begin. Someone said, perhaps the same, What possessed you to come? I could have stayed in my den, snug and dry, I couldn't. My den, I'll describe it, no, I can't. It's simple, I can do nothing any more, that's what you think. I say to the body, Up with you now, and I can feel it struggling, like an old hack **foundered** in the street, struggling no more, struggling **again**, till it gives up. I say to the head, Leave it alone, stay quiet, it stops **breathing**, then pants on worse than ever. I am **far from all** that wrangle, I shouldn't bother with it, I need nothing, neither to go on nor to stay where I am, it's truly all one to me, I should turn away from it all, away from the body, away from the head, let them work it out between them, let them cease, I can't, it's I would have to cease. **Ah yes**, we seem to be more than one, all deaf, not even **gathered** together for life. Another said, or the same, or the first, they all have the same voice, the same ideas, All you had to do was stay at home. Home. They wanted me to go home. My dwelling-place. But for the mist, with good eyes, with a telescope, I could see it from here. It's not just tiredness, I'm not just tired, **in** spite of the climb. It's not that I want to stay here either. I had heard tell, I must have heard tell of the view, the distant sea in **hammered** lead, the so-called golden vale so often sung, the **double valleys**, the glacial loughs, the city in its haze, it was all on every tongue.

the Croft Museum
Open Summer 10 am – 5 pm (Hours Might Differ)

Who are these people anyway? Did they follow me up here, go before me, come with me? I am **down in the hole the centuries** have dug, centuries of filthy weather, flat on my face on the dark earth sodden with the creeping saffron waters it slowly drinks. They are up **above, all round me, as in a graveyard.** I can't raise my eyes to them, what a pity, I wouldn't see their faces, their legs perhaps, plunged in the heath. Do they see me, what can they see of me? Perhaps there is no one left, perhaps they are all gone, sickened. I listen and it's the same thoughts I hear, I mean the same as ever, strange. To think in the valley the sun is blazing all down the ravelled sky. How long have I been here, what a question, I've often wondered. And often I could answer, An hour, a month, a year, a century, depending on what I mean by here, and me, and being, and there I never went looking for extravagant meanings, there I never much varied, only the here would sometimes seem to vary. Or I said, I can't have been here long, I wouldn't have held out. I hear the curlews, that means close of day, fall of night, for that's the way with curlews, silent all day, then crying when the darkness gathers, that's the way with those wild creatures and **so short-lived, compared to me.** And that other question I know so well too, What possessed you to come?

waiting for the ferry, Rousay

of the parts, fairly well, the cold is eating me, the wet too, at least I presume so, I'm far. My rheumatism in any case is no more than a memory, it hurts me no more than my mother's did, when it hurt her. Eye ravening patient in the haggard vulture face, perhaps it's carrion time. **I'm up here** and I'm down here, under my gaze, foundered, **eyes closed,** ear cupped against the sucking peat, we're of one mind, all of one mind, always were, deep down, we're fond of one another, we're sorry for one another, but there it is, there's **nothing we can do for** one another. One thing at least is certain, in **an hour** it will be too late, **in half-an-hour it will be night**, yet it's not, not certain, what is not certain, absolutely certain, that night prevents what day permits, for those who know how to go about it, who have the will to go about it, and the strength, the strength to try again. Yes. It will be night, **the mist will clear**. I know my mist. for all my distraction, **the wind freshen**, and the whole night sky open over **the mountain, with its lights**, including the Bears, to guide me once again on my way, let's wait for night. All mingles, times **and** tenses, at first I only had been here, now I'm here still, **soon I won't be here** yet, toiling up the slope, or in the bracken by the wood, it's larch, I don't try to understand, **I'll never** try to under- stand any more, that's what you think, for the moment I'm here, always **have been**, always shall be, I won't be afraid of the big words any more, they are not big. I don't remember coming, I can't go, all my little company, my eyes are closed and I feel the wet humus harsh against my cheek, my hat is gone, it can't be gone far, or the wind has swept it away, I was attached to it. Sometimes it's the sea, other times the mountains, often it was the forest, the city, the plain too, I've flirted with the plain too.

SPATE

At any moment, I might
stand up, walk outside
                cross the road to the
                              waterfall

teeter above its cold roar
   and spinning sticks, drenching gusts,
rainbows, and dive

      into the rushing, milky broil
of stone and fish and
sudden silence

      pull and kick
downstream through clouds of weed,
brown pools of light
        and thick earth crumbling;

surfacing wild-eyed to gasp

then dive down again,
        into the huge blue-black
                my river has become

      where it seeps into the sea
              and I dissolve,
a shadow in the salt, a green amongst greens

      a brief thickness below the keel
      of an Arbroath trawler,
felt through the heels of the skipper
whose brow momentarily furrows.

FEBRUARY
Montrose Basin

USAN
the sea leads through a gap in the dike,
down to a beach
where land begins to rise and fall.

ROSSIE MOOR
gradually, in listening, you empty
into the turf.
at last, here are the birds.

BODDIN
a curved boat
a curved, grey ocean.
the ocean, its continents of dark.

MOUND
stones ring
with the thump of cloud.
a blackbird, dead in flight.

DUN
among twenty snowy mountains,
the only moving thing
a windmill, blinking.

STREET
a phone is ringing:
birds whistle overhead,
whole trees full of words.

THE LURGIES
and three swans,
dropping out of the current,
muffling their wings.

FERRYDEN
an icebreaker is moored
between the houses.
a huge effort in this silence.

DYKE
a civil twilight.
the sun now below the hill,
the first stars just visible

STICKS BURN
a string of yellow lamps.
a hill burn, gulping down.
a deer lifting into the forest.

CROSSING THE PENTLAND

.
then suddenly the ocean sinks
where it rolls
against the surface

breaching, in daylight
with outbreaths of the real
cold sea.

it closes over
like time flowing backwards.

[silence]

THE VOYAGE OF THE 'FOX'
by Captain Francis L. McClintock. London: John Murray, 1859.

> Shall we follow?
> Quick, said the bird, find them, find them
> T.S. Eliot, *Burnt Norton*

i.
All birds are scarce,
the few retreating southward.

A raven was shot today; two eagles
at Bellot, a brace of willow grouse

our little auks the only birds remaining
in twos and ones – obscure, barely visible.

I was fortunate to shoot a snowy owl;
the flesh is tender white, but tasteless.

ii.
Our harmonium is on the lower deck.
The men enjoy its pleasing tones.

While Christian turns its handle,
stellar crystals fall:

they have six points
and in the sun or moonlight

glisten brilliantly;
our masts and rigging

a lace crust, brittle as glass
gorgeous, with no disruption.

iii.
A white whale was shot yesterday:
a female of ordinary dimensions
a fine cream colour
her eyes extremely small;

the steaks of her flesh divide
like seal, though not as tender;
her orifices scarcely large enough
to admit a quill.

      *

And there, at the sudden run
from glassy blue to mud –

white whales
obscured, like lumps in milk.

>*a ship*
>*a brother in our trade*
>*a joy in these barren regions.*

*

Upernivik, 17th May 1858
And Mrs Olrik, at home
in her heated parlour,
her bright windows full of sun:

her scented cambric
her lilac, roses, mignonette
profusion of geranium.

iv.
Our magnetic observations have begun,
our ice house just large enough
to hold the declinometer.

Soon Hobson will leave us
for the Pole, advancing our depots
charting our half knowledge of these vast

superficies of thin, young ice
and gusts of rain, and silence.
I do not envy him.

v.
This island is covered in native marks
one stone standing on another

the outer stones weathered pale,
the newer stones bleached and flattened

by centuries of rough light.
There is great doubt arriving at their meaning:

a monument, a fixed point
holding earth and sky together

the hills of their eyes worn down
like old men, weathered into silence

their story no longer remote,
this island, and the ocean outside.

> close down to the beach, and the other higher up, examining the more conspicuous parts: in this order we traversed the remaining portion of the island.
> Although the snow served to conceal from us any traces which might exist in hollows or sheltered situations, yet it rendered all objects intended to serve as marks proportionably conspicuous; and we may remember that it was in its winter garb that the retreating crews saw Montreal Island, precisely as we ourselves saw it. The island was almost covered with native marks, usually of one stone standing upright upon another, sometimes consisting of three stones, but very rarely of a greater number.

a harbour filled with sunlight;
then a cloud passes
and the harbour is empty.

vi.
We march at night, towards
the dark of southern latitudes

and take our meals by lamplight
in silence, drunk with sleep.

Yesterday, the aurora loured above us
burning salt green, electrical

windless and flickering
cloaking the horizon till dawn

then hovering, hoarse and silvery
like low fog, freezing our instruments

our compasses now useless.
Without them we are blind as kittens.

vii.
We are drifting freely from the shore
further and further
on fresh growths of ice.

I pass the time adding to our charts:
the thin grey headlands
scree and hollow

the blank
unenchanted islands,
their tiny black rivers inked in.

My pen lifts them from the darkness.

viii.   *23rd July*
the Moravian settlement:
a dull red house
a belfry, a dozen native huts.

Petersen pulled aside a membrane
of some animal, which guarded against the wind
but admitted light,

even past midnight. There was
the human music of
low conversation, some small dance songs.

A boy brought us a handful of garnets.

a book of Christian melodies
a pencil
a scent of grass.

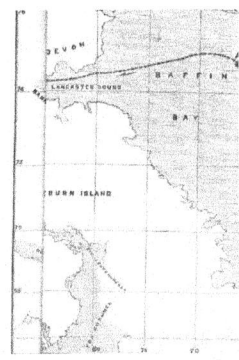

ix.   *54°21'50"N*
Brisk and west:
cold with a sense of beyond.

Our sense of gloom has lifted:
the men have ample occupation,
disfigured as they are by the sun and

bright cold winds.
They do not like alluding to the dead,
their ordinary senses more suited

to moving with the weather
further south, where places overlap

or hauling through the Pentland Firth
the hoarse screams of the pilot
his dialect the shrill cry of sea birds,
as if we were in Greenland itself –

LITTORAL   rune poems

'The text commonly called the Icelandic rune-poem is only a poem by courtesy'.
    R.I. Page, Viking Society for Northern Research, 1999.

coriolis   a deflection
                                a drift to the east
                                a north sea sun chill

littoral   talus – a debris
                                the friction of the shore
                                a memory, a dull prehension

amphidrome   a null point,
                                an upwelling. a stealth,
                                approaching from all directions

crail   its sea dip
                                its reds and underwater greens
                                its blinking windows

macula   larval, eel-like
                                a form beneath the surface
                                a pitting between cells

BIRDS OF ANGUS

from *The Agriculture of Angus or Forfarshire*,
by the Rev. James Headrick, Minister of Dunichen. 1813.

Scolopax arquata	the mountain curlew
Charadrius himantopus	the long-legged plover
Emberiza nivalis	the snow flake
Falco milvus	the gled
Falco pygargus	the ring tail
Falco gentilis	the gentle falcon
Emberiza citrinella	the yaldring
Hirundo rustica	the chimney swallow
Ampelis garrulus	the chatterer
Falco albicilla	the erne
Sterna hirundo	the sea swallow
Tringa cinclus	the purre
Motacilla salicaria	the reed sparrow
Motacilla trochilus	the yellow wren
Parus ater	the coal mouse
Larus tridactylus	the tarrock
Haematopus ostralegus	the seapie
Larus hybernus	the winter gull

VOTIVE SHIPS

> The annals say: when the monks of Clonmacnoise
> Were all at prayers inside the oratory
> A ship appeared above them in the air.
>   Seamus Heaney, *Lightenings*

i.   *16th century graffiti, Bassingham*

    a thin ship
    gradual, becoming
    between traffic and leaf-still

    sailing
    in stone coloured twilight
    the inner world and the outer deep.

ii.   *St Monans Kirk, Fife*

    or this morning at the shoreline:
    a new front, dim and uncertain

    draining all colour from the air
    until the horizon had vanished

    our small boats hanging, suspended
    between earth and sky – vaprous, almost air

       neither steersman nor tiller
       in sea gleam, in still bright water.

iii.   *Oude Kerk, Amsterdam*

       stirring
       between pole and tropic,

       these dark boats
       that glide in thought, mid ocean

       like birds, their swiftness of intellect
       their clean sharp flight

       through steep walls
       and odd parts of sunlight.

iv.   the *Chloe* GY11, Grimsby Fishing Heritage Centre

       the tide rolls in
       slithering off pilings

       dragging under;
       the blurt of drains, the sudden sump of pavements

our sea streets
flowing inland, on half bright hills

where you and I are
held to the world.

vi.   *Århus Cathedral, Denmark*

a shallow bowl,
its threads lengthened for attention

self contained, its slope and weight
displacing the world around it.

how near we are to the world;
the draw of these sudden towns

their cars and footfall,
their tall wood houses that creak

as the turf beneath them dries, subsiding.
its underside shimmers like a leaf.

THURSDAY POEM

All afternoon, she opens
her eyelids, stretching yellow limbed,
her body slipping water, the lichen's slow explosions spreading

like barnacles. The tide runs through her thighs,
saline and dull, black with eels that slick into her side
where she is frayed like an anemone. It was

like opening a door. The water pressed her down
shoulders first, beneath the cockle shelf where clouds of sperm
seeped through her hair, her muscle tongue
retreating, words fluttering in the sand, digging in.

Now she mouths her own astonished O
at the flood that will wash her clean again: her broken
nails, her still, lovely face full of joy, swallowing.

CROVIE

i.
at fraserburgh, surfers
dip through the curl –
black in green, black in white

ii.
memsie – cardno – coburty
lochlip – towie
clintery – quithle – troup

iii.
all day, the sun setting;
each crest a long plume,
each trough a dark tunnel.

iv.
three dark birds
wide winged, squat and folded
wait above the wrack

v.
vent and flue open.
vent open, flue shut, damper.
vent shut, flue open.

vi.
Force Six.
the air turns white
the necklace of white lamps blotted out.

vii.
in the back yard, on bare cement
five sanderlings,
water-white and mute

viii.
flue shut, vent open
damper and flue shut open
vent and flue shut. wood.

ix.
in the early hours
fresh in from the north,
the sea rattling at the door.

x.
all sound is the wind
all sound is the sea outside
all sound is the wind

DECEMBER, SKAGASTRÖND

During the many months of making these interviews I learned something important about Iceland, about voices, about the weather … I cannot say exactly, but it's connected with people's different ways of dwelling on the moment, reading their environment and the people around them.
  Oddný Eir Ævarsdóttir, *Weather Reports You*

.

midwinter:
when sunrise and sunset are the same
one hour   then another

in minutely changing detail –
orange   orange, red

each note growing longer,
holding its tone

the hills behind gleaming
the sea a wordless green

.

monday.
swimming through daylight
holding the moon in my head

I stretch my arms to show
how wide, how thin
the flow of cold air from

these elongated mountains
the road splaying out at the sea,
the sea's pitted surface.

.
morning.
daylight is a whitewash

of seaweed under cars,
and land voices on the pier
and huddled boats, each in its own black halo.
the tide is viscous, like tar.

low cloud.

a flat acoustic ceiling;
the crane and winch, hammering
the edges of the sea to the beach.

the shop's electric door that
bleats across the car park.

.
night-time:
a hail of charged particles streams
from the pole

an ice blue sail,
riffling in draughts
mineral   amorphous

receding upwards
in a fine gauze screen.

the heat of the television –
its tropical colours
lapping at the ceiling.

.

rain falls,
a light / dense pattern
a soft pandemonium

a conscious   fingertip beating
slowly going out of phase
as the cloud blows over.

air over grass,
wind over water.

.

Sunday – low tide.
gulls pick relics from the beach,
tinkering with molluscs

pattering triangles
into black   thick mud.

a tiny agnostic piece of ice
floats out / in
warped, like concrete.

.

lull.

how the wind crumples
between houses,

a momentary trough
that allows quiet in.

slight turbulence,
like walking through a mirror.

.

Saturday.
hitching at the roadside

the steady hiss of rain
the mountain eroding, molecule by molecule.

a warm day, midwinter.
memorous insects
are humming and swaying

tightened into knots
in pockets of low damp
heat, and wan sunlight.

slight ecstasies of moths.

LIZZIE FAIRY
Elizabeth Fairweather, b. 1857, Auchmithie.

lizzie fairy, dellin doon
eassan onder at the shore
water white an shallow green
pickin dulse an carrageen

lizzie fairy, pewlie gull
threidin fishes by the tail
drawin water fae the well
drawin wither fae the sea

lizzie fairy at the door
hingin washin in the air
sheilin mussels on the moon
coorie up an coorie doon

lizze fairy, cool an deid
bunnelled roon in turf an weed
swallow dip in barley rain
rowan bed an thistle seed

dellin / delving   *eassan onder* / east and yonder
pewlie gull / calling gull   *sheilin* / shelling

HESSLE ROAD

~

so I went fishing out of Spain
                round the south end of England   the Irish coast
                                                                                       hake, whiting

then the Falklands, fishing for squid
                you had to pick the horn out
          we were flown home with the ship

I came home   went casualling on the fish dock.
    It's the sea life more than anything
    I've done nothing else but the sea

~

        well he said you can tie a cod line can't you
        well he said you've been doin as third hand
                            so we let go and sailed

~

we went to the North Sea and places like that
we went to Ireland and Ullapool, transferring
we went to Wales and left the ship
we went to Wales and took the bus home

~

mackerel is just a thing:

                      you come across a **mark**
                      you tow across the **mark**
                                  that hole
                      and the boat would be full

~

              he tried hard to come home.
when they turned the ship round to come back

          we knew before most people

if the tides were right, we went to meet him
                                    the ship coming in at the dock.

but at the back of that,
there was that worry, like when another ship went down
        and you'd be anxious until they came.   there was
            always his suit in the wardrobe
            always his shirts pressed

~

or tugs and supply boats –
like driving a taxi,
always on standby

or tied up in Peterhead:
handle an anchor, move a rig,
back in

~

water - fish slab - floating ice - the bobbers landing kits - board scrubbers - the cod liver oil, pumping out - I've no sort of clear cut - shore riggers splicing wires - the Marconi man - coal wagons, clankerin an clankerin, bunkerin the ships up - miles and miles of coal -

~

2 am: the bobbers
walking to work in their clogs
iron shod, like horses

or barra lad, a hundred kit in yer barra:
        run there
        run back
        run there
        run back

or the women
at tide time, blowing kisses

or the women at night
mending nets out back

~

    pulling and riving　　　　　　a second honeymoon –
    using the wind,　　　　　　　two or three days
    the fish put away in minutes,　a day for each week

    it was part of our play –　　　a village:
        ships alongside,　　　　　four thousand fishermen at sea.
        meet your daddy,　　　　I was there before I was born

~

    at sixty two, I did a trip pleasuring
                          fresh fishing – the norwegian coast –
       thirteen days twelve hours, dock to dock
                 the grounds that I used to
         I've never felt so well

~

   the last haul, going home:
       the watch stopped
       all hands for six
             to get the back broken of the work

   twenty men on deck
   and everything else is forgotten

HULL

Swing the lamp:
four loud voices
like a layer of oil on the
table.

the bulla (n):
i. a mollusc with thin, fragile shells
ii. of whales, the middle ear–

evening air:
the offshore breeze
spilling over the horizon.

Balaena mysticetus
   the whale,
      its human gasps

  – Sunk Sands – North Channel –
  – Hawke Road – Sunk Spit – Foul
  Holme – Paull Sands - Paull End –

a breach –
the buss, a wet lobe
plosive, exhaling

at the horizon
a ship, inverted
sailing on its masts

lux, candela:
  a visible light, near green
  pure spermacetti

  a cloud bank,
  the sea ice-green
  glittering like the ice cap

the Gulf Stream –
a blue streak, entirely transparent.
a sleeve of glass.

hoisted
foetal, collapsing
in its own sudden weight

[Blacktoft Jetty]
  light, occulting
  a conscious, constant I

duntie – æður – eidereend
mallimak – maali – qaqulluk
redshank – stelkur – tureluur

– Symmetry – Thomas –
Thornton – Trafalgar –
Truelove – Valentine –
Venerable – Zephyr –

old Truelove,
staunch and true.
Peace to her ashes.

– Keddington –
– Langled – Rough –
–Dan – Tyra – Roar – Valhall –

ENGLAND - RIVER HUMBER
King George Dock   53° 44.4′ No° 16.4′ W
Entrance, E.   **Oc.Bu.**
                      period 5s

old Harmony,
rounded in chains.

Whitby to The Wash
Wind *F3 SE becoming SSE*
Max. Gust *17kn becoming 15kn*
Sea State *Smooth becoming Slight*
Visibility *Good*

                      the White Sea.

[MAERSK]
  continents adjust
  in a dark, closed room

  a tremor,
  a sound moving off

Fresh way. – Increased speed
      through the water.

[Spurn Point]
  sunset.
  whole cities slide by
  weightless, inverted

  fog –
  a peculiar blackness
  a mid-morning silence.

from Ronas Voe,
poor drowned sailors
walking home across the sky

Flurry. – The convulsive
   movement of a dying
   whale.

        – St MAGNUS GROUND –
   TURBOT BANK *Rough* – OTTER
      BANK SPRING & SUMMER
  HALIBUT.COD.LING. WHEN CLEAR OF
            DOGFISH

[twilight]
  the pilot boat hurries out –
  a turbulence of small lights
  a wash of surface noise

     December -
Breiðafjörður, Faxaflöi
sucking your fingers to your elbow

The watch:
  18 hours on
  6 below

   Those lost at sea
  come back as birds.

  Fisc flodu ahoft
  this-fish the-tide
  raised (i.e. stranded)

OUTER BAILEY
  a dozen petrels
  low to the water

  on ferenberig
  onto mountain-mound
  (i.e. ashore);

or the women
at tide time, blowing kisses

or the women at night
mending nets out back

land light:
  its hoodwink eye
  unblinking

  • • •
  • • •
• • • •
  • • •

  sīc *(Old English)*
  sík *(Old Norse)*
  sig *(Danish)*
  sike *(Yorkshire)*
  syke *(Berwick)*

DISAPPEARANCE

> [29th January]
> *I must have disturbed him when I came up the companion
> … He was unapproachable, as a misfit should be.*
> – Donald Crowhurst, logbook of the
> Teignmouth Electron

[…]
How, singlehanding in a bad storm,
light-poor, deprived of sleep, beyond isolation

and fatigue as the boat took a beating
shedding green tons, letting the dark in

through shuddering deck boards;
working at waking, the tiller jammed hard

at his side while the boat leaned and leaned,
the second up front, watching the sea's sliding surface

as it brimmed and fell while he nursed the boat across
great holes that closed and opened

beside them, the two of them watching for minutes
as the storm fretted and at last began

to fail, the boat butting forward, correcting its roll
in small calms, riding weightless

as the surface formed
itself and held, the wind sighing

in one vast outbreath,
and then he was alone again.

[…]
clutch and cling –
through boiling green
the bow thrusts down

upheaving rainbows,
a figure distorted
in the spume

nudging the boat
along, *our wake
behind tumbling*

[25th December]

0430	Nil	GKL
0435	Nil	GKT
0440	Nil	GKL
0450	Nil	GKH
0527	*Sighs heard*	

[10th July]
ghosting:
a purely mental pleasure

the boat, or his body
compelled forward

the helm swinging freely,
the undertow

slowing down / enlarging
lifting him

out of the world
into brightness,

himself at the centre of this
infinite space.

[24th June]   *17.739 mhz Radio Wolna Europa*
hysterical laughter
(private note)

[13th November]
Today, some reel to reel recording.
my voice makes a room of itself:
the cabin fills with listening.

Outside, the seagulls;
their needy

        I am   I am

[5th November]
picking up the South East Trades
an old clipper route
getting well to the west.

a whaler, French or Spanish

[23rd June]
– four rudimentary limbs,
and on the end of each, a further eight
small hands, each coral finger turned

back on itself. And with
a most delicate and beautiful colouring –
silver and blue, almost translucent

pale pink beneath.
My presence seemed to touch off something
that glimmered though his skin

flowering in numerous tiny extrusions
along the lobes of its spines,
the green becoming more intense, the bluish more brilliant,

his shape approaching simple perfection
as if revolved on a compass –
every fingery detail splayed beneath

my god-like vision.
                    Perhaps it was the sun:
all afternoon I watched as he waned

growing smaller and weaker, retracting into himself,
becoming more and more private
until I realised he had gone.

Such was our brief companionship.

[22nd June]
entering the calms:
the Horse Latitudes.

the sun shines, benign.

there is a whale.
there is a cloud.

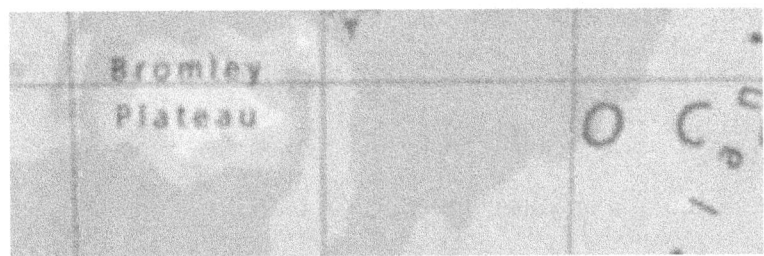

[6th March]
land light:
its hoodwink eye
unblinking.,

[23rd June]
almost voices:
high up near the bridge
gazing down

at this tiny figure
sailing out of earshot.

[…]
Do I see him?

a trace or
forward memory /
a figment of exhaustion

a lone sailor,
helming the boat
by fragments and signs,

brown hooded
turning off, already
half erased

the swirling sea
drawn round him.

[…]
heading north:

the sky disordered,
the sea
cold green, uneasy

always now
with its straining,
its sliding off

the tall sky empty
the tall sky empty.

[23rd June]
sailing closer,
nearing the horizon.

its fogs are translucent
*– colour without form
and I am lost, entirely*

*free of the condition of
a body in space*

[...]
starlight
a bare, bright realm
of unhindered logic

[...]
the night sky
a long bright silence.

its brute structures
make the world visible,
allowing soul to wander

abstract, homeless
and strangely at peace.

On 31st October 1968, Donald Crowhurst set out to circumnavigate the globe in his one-man trimaran. Nine months later, the boat was found abandoned.

BURNHEAD

*The Mawse Burn, which drains what was once The Meadows, runs
under the pavement outside the Registry Office in Dundee.*

in the pavement sump, in the sudden dry blurt in plug holes
in the well gait, the quaw bog, the bitter burn; in logie spout, in meadow side
in the fingery creep of damp, in inky stairwells buckled with snails
in an old sea cave, welling and sinking with the tide
in blurred holes of slime and kelp, flooding uphill and disappearing like a storm
in the mill dam, drained of itself, throttled and glugging in a cellar
in a blue lick, a brown vein; an isobathic stream of air;
a cool current in a room; a line where we hold hands, and step over.

notes

Birds of the North Sea was published in *Landscapes: Journal of the International Centre for Landscapes and Language*; **Close's Fishermen's Map** in *English*; **Orkney Road Trip with Samuel Beckett** in *Try to be Better [an engagement with W.S. Graham]*, ed. S. Buchan-Watts & L. Singer (Prototype, 2019); **February, Montrose Basin** in *Forty Voices Strong: an Anthology of Contemporary Scottish Poetry* ed. P. Moran (Grayson, 2019); **Lizzie Fairy** in *The Antigonish Review*. An earlier version of **The Voyage of the 'Fox'** appeared in *The Dalhousie Review*. It includes quotations from T.S. Eliot's *Four Quartets*.

Birds of Angus and **Burnhead** were written for Making Space for Water, a cross-disciplinary project funded by Creative Scotland and Scottish Natural Heritage. **December, Skagaströnd** was written during a Nes Artists Residency in north-west Iceland.

The photograph on p.43 is of a mural by Guido van Helten, one of two which he painted in the town of Skagaströnd in 2013. The face is of a crew member from a visiting fishing boat. The images interspersed with the text in 'The Voyage of the Fox' are from an Elibron reproduction of McClintock's published journal. The image on p.54 is from Bas Jan Ader's exhibition *In Search of the Miraculous*; the photograph on p.56 was taken by Frank Hermann of *The Sunday Times*. All other images are my own.

HULL: Images from APB Humber Estuary Services *Current Humber Charts*; JNCC *Directory Of The North Sea Coastal Margin*, distribution of white-beaked dolphin. Quotations from *Close's Fishermen's Chart of the North Sea*; OED; BBC Shipping Forecast; Franks Casket rune translated by Bill Griffith.

www.ingramcontent.com/pod-product-compliance
Lightning Source LLC
Chambersburg PA
CBHW080407170426
43193CB00016B/2843